Blake's GO GUIDES

EVERYDAY MATHS

Pauline Rogers

PASCAL
PRESS

Copyright © Pascal Press 2004

ISBN 1 874125 043 9

Pascal Press
PO Box 250
Glebe NSW 2037
(02) 8585 4044
www.pascalpress.com.au

Publisher: Vivienne Petris Joannou
Editor: Jane Tyrrell
Page design, layout and cover by DiZign Pty Ltd
Photo research by Tracey Gibson
Photos by Ingram Publishing, PhotoDisc, Rubberball, www.photos.com,
www.photospin.com.
Printed in Australia by Printing Creations

A NOTE FROM THE PUBLISHER

In our world we use maths every day. Managing our money, buying and selling property, doing the shopping and choosing a mobile phone plan all involve the use of maths. The better we understand the processes involved in everyday mathematics, the better we can meet our needs and wants. By improving our understanding of the maths we encounter every day, we can make the wisest decisions with our personal finances. With this simple guide you can improve your basic maths understanding and skills, an improvement that will pay dividends each and every day.

As with all our Go Guides we aim to bring you the greatest amount of really useful information in the shortest number of pages. After all, who has time to read 300-page books on basic mathematics? So, this book is designed to give you quick access to the information and skills you need to know without the padding that so many self-help books contain.

If you have any comments on how this book could be improved, please do not hesitate to email me at matthew@pascalpress.com.au.

Matthew Blake
Publisher

ABOUT THE AUTHOR

Pauline Rogers has had a long-time involvement in the teaching of mathematics. In addition to years of primary and secondary experience, she has worked in the tertiary sector as an education officer. She holds a postgraduate qualification in Information Technology and a Masters in Science and currently works for the Mathematics Association of Victoria.

TABLE OF CONTENTS

INTRODUCTION

Each day you use some form of mathematics. It is everywhere and is relevant to so many things. From the moment you wake up, maths is there — it is the clock and the time, the amount of breakfast cereal you eat, the volume of milk you put in your coffee, the distance you travel to work and the cost of fuel. It is the amount of money spent at the supermarket, the percentage discount received and how much tax you pay. The list is endless.

Blake's Go Guide: Everyday Maths equips you with simple explanations and gives many examples of areas in which maths appears in your day-to-day life. It explores the areas of currency and shopping, time and phone calls. The guide examines your money and what you are paying in tax, superannuation and the mathematics behind investment. There is information about car calculations, including buying a car, fuel for a trip and the time it takes to travel a particular distance. You'll find it can help you with the application of mathematics to property, including buying and selling as well as renovating.

The guide provides you with a quick reference in areas that involve mathematics. It is designed to give you the basic skills to complete calculations and further your understanding of some of the mathematics that you often encounter.

BUYING PROPERTY

Financing a property

When buying a property there are a number of options for financing the purchase.

$100 000 loan

Interest rate (% p.a.)	Monthly repayments over period of loan (assuming fixed rate)		
	15 years	20 years	25 years
6.25%	$857	$731	$660
6.50%	$871	$746	$675
6.75%	$885	$760	$691
7.00%	$927	$806	$739

$200 000 loan

Interest rate (% p.a.)	Monthly repayments over period of loan (assuming fixed rate)		
	15 years	20 years	25 years
6.50%	$1742	$1479	$1350
6.75%	$1770	$1521	$1382
7.00%	$1854	$1611	$1478

Source: *Blake's Go Guide: Buying and Selling Real Estate.*

Types of loans

Loans can be:

- **fixed interest rate**: where the same amount is paid for the life of the loan and there may be penalties for paying out the loan earlier.
- **variable rate**: where the interest rate will vary throughout the life of the loan. For example, for the $200 000 loan in the table above, you may start paying off the loan at 6.75%, which equates to $1382 per month for 25 years; however, 2 years into the loan, the rates drop to 6.25%, so you will now be paying $1319 per month.
- **combination loans**: where part of the mortgage is fixed and the other is variable. More details are provided in *Blake's Go Guide: Buying and Selling Real Estate.*

Most lenders, as a rule, require a minimum deposit of 10% of the purchase price.

Working out the deposit

To work out how much deposit you'll have to pay:

Purchase price × 10/100 = Deposit

For example: For a home that costs $320 000, you will be required to have at least:

$320 000 × 10/100 = $32 000
purchase price   **the percentage**   **deposit**

Working out the setup costs

When buying a property there are a number of set up costs which usually add up to approximately 5% of the purchase price. These include:

- stamp duty on purchase price
- stamp duty on the mortgage
- solicitor's/conveyancer's fees ($600–$2500)
- mortgage application fee
- valuation fee ($150–$250)
- mortgage insurance
- building inspection ($250–$400)
- pest inspection ($150–$250).

To work out how much to allow for set up costs

Purchase price × 5/100 = Total amount

$320 000 × 5/100 = $16 000
purchase price   **the percentage**   **total amount**

Working out the upfront and ongoing expenses

As well as the loan repayments and set up costs, other immediate expenses include:

- home insurance
- council rates
- water rates
- removalist fees
- connection of phone, gas and electricity.

There are a number of websites to help you tally up these expenses. The following table was created using the web site: www.yourmortgage.com.au

Location

State	VIC
Region	Major city

Property and mortgage information

House price	$320 000
Mortgage amount	$300 000
Term of loan	25 years
Interest rate	6.25%
Loan to value ratio (LVR)	93.75%

Upfront costs

Deposit amount	$20 000
Stamp duty on loan	$1164
Stamp duty on property	$14 860
Transfer fees	$877
Mortgage insurance	$4710
Telephone connection	$50
Building report	$250
Pest report	$150
Solicitor's/conveyancer's fees	$1000
Mortgage application fee	$200
Removalist costs	$4800
Total upfront costs	**$48 061**

Ongoing monthly costs

Loan repayment	$1979
Home and contents insurance	$50
Rates	$46
Total monthly ongoing costs	**$2075**

Note: If you borrow more than 70–80% of the property's value you will need mortgage protection insurance.

More details regarding the main points can be found in *Blake's Go Guide: Buying and Selling Real Estate.*

SELLING PROPERTY

When selling a property there are some costs that need to be taken into account. These could include:

Independent valuer	$150–$250
Agent's commission	2–5% of the sale price
Property 'make-over'	1–5% of the property value
Solicitors/conveyancer's fee	$600–$2500
Advertising and auction costs	costs vary
Early mortgage discharge fee	costs vary

For example:

A property which sold for $175 000 incurred the following costs:

Selling price	$175 000
Independent valuer	$175
Agent's commission	3% (3/100 × $175 000 = $5250)
Solicitor's fee	$1250
Amount received	$168 325

Working out your profit

To work out your net profit:

Amount received − (Initial purchase price + Additional expenses)
= Net profit

If the property was initially purchased for $150 000 and the owners spent $7500 fixing and repairing the property then the net profit would be:

$168 325   –   ($150 000   + $7500)   = $10 825
amount received   initial purchase price   additional expenses =   net profit

More details are provided in *Blake's Go Guide: Buying and Selling Real Estate*.

INVESTING IN PROPERTY

Property is a long-term investment and depends on the market. It requires investors to carry mortgages of hundreds of thousands of dollars, and you cannot sell off a bedroom if you need fast cash.

There are tax benefits for the investor but outgoings would need to be considered.

Calculating your loan repayments

To work out your loan repayments
Monthly loan repayments × number of months
= Total annual loan repayments

An investment property is purchased for $225 000. If the property is purchased with a loan of $200 000 for 25 years at 6.5% interest per annum, with monthly payments of $1290, then total repayments per year would be:

$1350   ×   12   = $15 480
monthly loan repayments   **no of months**   **total annual loan repayments**

Working out your net return

A good rule of thumb is to deduct 25% of the gross rental to account for outgoings such as rates, insurance, maintenance.
For example:

To work out your net return:
Total income – Total expenses = Net return

The investment property is rented at $400 per week, making the annual rent $20 800 ($400 × 52).

$20 800 ×   25/100   = $5200
annual rent   the percentage   total expenses

To calculate the net return before tax relief:

$20 800   – $5200   = $15 600
total income   **total expenses**   **net return**

After all expenses are deducted, but before tax incentives, the property's net return would be:

$15 600   – $15 480   = $120
net return after expenses deducted   annual loan repayments   new net return

Working out how much the property has increased in value

The net return doesn't include the increase in property value, for example, the same property is in a fast growing area, and after 5 years property prices have increased by 15%.

Working out the property's increase in value
Initial cost of property × Percentage increase/100 = Amount of increase

The property is now worth:

$225 000   ×   15/100   = $33 750
initial cost of property   percentage increase   amount of increase

To work out the new value of property:
Cost of property + Amount of increase = New value of property

$225 000   + $33 750   = $258 750
initial cost of property   amount of increase   new value of property

Along with the $120 net return per year for 5 years, the investment has returned a total of:

$33 750 + (5 × $120) = $34 350 before tax incentives.

Note: The above assumes that both the rental income and the interest rate on the loan stay the same over the 5-year period.

Depreciation

Depreciation is a percentage of the cost of the item, claimed as a deduction on the assets that you own which are used to produce an income, i.e. fixtures or fittings in a rental property or equipment at a plant.

Working out depreciation on the asset

To calculate the total depreciation of an asset the original cost of the item needs to be noted, then the effective life of the item needs to be estimated.

To work out how much depreciation you can claim:
**Days held / 365 × 1 / Effective life of the item in years × Cost of asset
= Total depreciation**

For example:

If you have curtains in a rental property worth $1000 with an effective life of 10 years then you could claim $100 per year for 10 years.

$$\underset{\text{days held}}{365/365} \times \underset{\text{effective life of item in years}}{1/10} \times \underset{\text{cost of asset}}{\$1000} = \underset{\text{total depreciation}}{\$100}$$

Thus the full price of the curtains could be claimed over 10 years.

Note: if you sell the item, as in this example the property with the curtains, at a profit this is fine but you will need to pay tax on that amount. More information can be found in *Blake's Go Guide: Tax and You*.

Negative gearing

Negative gearing occurs when you buy an income-producing property and the deductible costs of ownership exceed the assessable income.

Working out what deductions can you claim

With a rental property you can claim a number of deductions including:

- interest paid on the loan to acquire the property
- agent's costs of finding tenants or managing the property
- rates
- repairs and maintenance (not improvements)
- depreciation of fixtures and fittings or possibly the building itself.

For example:

If you borrowed $100 000 at a fixed interest rate of 7.00% (loan period 25 years) to buy an income-producing property (purchase price $150 000) and received an annual rent of $9000 from the property, you could claim the following annual expenses in the first year:

Interest payments ($739 × 12 = $8868):	$8868
Agent's fees	$200
Land rates	$700
Painting the bathroom	$1000
Depreciation of carpets	$500
Building depreciation (at 2.5%)	$3750
Total deductions	**$15 018**

To work out the amount of loss or gain:

Income − Deductions = Total claimable loss/gain

For the example above you can claim a tax loss of $5700:

$$\underset{\text{income}}{\$9000} - \underset{\text{deductions}}{\$15\ 400} = \underset{\text{total claimable loss}}{-\$6400}$$

Note: this example includes GST in the overall prices.

RENOVATING YOUR HOUSE

Flooring
Working out the area

To calculate the cost of replacing flooring, first you need to work out the area of the space to be covered.

To calculate surface area:
Length × Width = Area

For example:
  Your kitchen floor is the shape of the diagram below:

8 metres

Shape 1

2 metres

4 metres

Shape 2   5 metres

4 metres

To work out the area of an irregular shape:
Area of shape 1 + Area of shape 2 = Total area

To work out the area of the diagram above:
The shaded area is 4m × 2m = 8m²
　　　　　　　　length width　area of shape 1

The unshaded area is 4m × 7m = 28m²
　　　　　　　　length width　area of shape 2

The total area is 8m² + 28m² = 36 m²
　　　area of shape 1　area of shape 2　total area

Working out the cost of materials

> To work out the cost of materials:
>
> **Area × Cost per square metre = Total cost of flooring materials**

To cover the floor with a timber, say Blackbutt 175mm x 22mm (T&G and end matched) at $87.00 per m², it would cost:

36m² × $87.00   = $3132.00.
area   **cost per square metre**   **total cost of flooring materials**

Note: this example includes GST in the overall prices.

Window coverings

To calculate the cost of window coverings, you need to measure the window space.

When looking at blinds such as timber venetians there are two measurement options:

1 Outside mounted or face fixed blinds (where the blind covers the whole area)

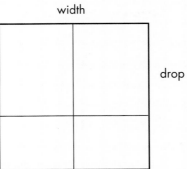

width

drop

2 Inside mount or recess fix blinds (where the blind fits into the window space).

In both cases, the width and the drop of the window need to be measured, and these should be in millimetres. For the outside mounted blinds, you need to measure beyond the window space for the covering. With the inside mounted blinds you need to ensure there is space for cords and the mechanisms to work.

Working out the cost of window coverings

To work out the cost of window coverings:

**Cost per blind × Number of blinds required
= Total cost of window coverings**

Example 1: You have 5 windows you want to cover with timber venetians. The measurement of the windows is 2100mm width and 600mm drop. The cost of the blinds is $79.99 each, making a total cost of $399.95,

$79.99   ×   5   = $399.95
cost per blind   no of blinds required   total cost of window coverings

With softer coverings, such as curtains, you also have outside mounts or inside mounts depending on the style of windows. With outside mounts, it may be desirable for the curtains to fall well below the window and this needs to be taken into consideration with the measurements.

Example 2: If you had decided to cover the windows (drop 2130mm by 900mm wide) with pre-made curtains, at a cost of $85.00 per set of curtains, then the total cost would be:

$85   ×   5   = $425.00
cost per blind   no of blinds required   total cost of window coverings

Working out the contractor costs

You could complete the renovating work yourself or have a contractor come in.

To work out the total contractor costs:

Cost per hour × Number of hours = Total contractor costs

Note: a contractor would include GST in their costs and this would be shown separately.

Example 1: If laying the wooden floor takes 6 hours at approximately $40 per hour, the cost of hiring a contractor would be $240 for the laying:

$40.00   ×   6   = $240.00
cost per hour   no of hours   total contractor costs

Example 2: A landscape gardener costing $44.00 per hour takes 50 hours to complete a garden, so his total costs would be:

$44.00   ×   50   = $2200
cost per hour   no of hours   total contractor costs

Note: this total does not include materials.

Working out the combined costs of the contractor and materials

To work out the total cost of the job:

Cost of flooring materials + Cost of contractor = Total cost

To work out the total cost of the job, the contractor costs need to be added to the cost of, in this case, the flooring materials:

$3132.00   + $240.00   = $3372.00
cost of flooring materials   cost of contractor   total cost

Note: a contractor would include GST in their costs and the cost of materials.

Working out call out fees

Generally tradespersons charge a call out fee and a per hour fee.

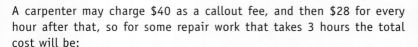

To work out the total cost including call out fee:

Callout fee + (Cost per hour × Hours taken) = Total cost

A carpenter may charge $40 as a callout fee, and then $28 for every hour after that, so for some repair work that takes 3 hours the total cost will be:

$40.00   +   ($28.00 × 3)   = $124.00
call out fee   cost per hour × number of hours   total cost

Working out the discounted amount

There may be a discount offered in certain cases, say, for paying cash.

To work out the total cost after the discount:

Total cost − (Total cost × Percentage discount/100)
= Discounted amount

If the carpenter gives a 10% discount the cost will now be:

$124.00 −   ($124.00 × 10/100)   = $111.60
total cost   total cost × percentage discount/100   discounted amount

INVESTING IN SHARES

Shares have the potential to provide better returns than other major investments as a long-term investment. When you buy shares in a company, you are buying a part of that company. This means that you share in the company's performance in the form of profits which can be given to you as dividends and/or capital growth through the value of your shares increasing. Buying and selling shares can cost as little as $15 for a transaction-only service.

Most share funds return about 10%, while others produce returns of over 40% in a 12-month period. However, some lose money and in this case a loss would be made.

Working out the share dividend amount

To work out the amount of dividend:

Amount invested × Percentage return/100 = Dividend amount

For a $15 000 investment in a company that returns 9% in a year, you will receive a dividend payment of:

$$\underset{\text{amount invested}}{\$15\ 000} \times \underset{\text{percentage return/100}}{9/100} = \underset{\text{dividend amount}}{\$1350}$$

For the same investment over a 5-year period, if the company returns on average 19% per year, and the dividends are added back into the total,

To work out the dividend amount over a period of time:

Investment amount $(1 + \text{rate per time interval}/100)^{\text{number of time intervals}}$ = Total amount

In our example above, the total amount would be:

$$\underset{\text{amount invested}}{\$15\ 000} \times \underset{(1\ +\ \text{rate per time interval})}{(1 + 19/100)^5} = \underset{\text{total amount}}{\$35\ 795.30}$$

Note: tax must be paid on dividends as they are a form of income.

SHORT TERM INVESTING IN FINANCIAL INSTITUTIONS

Term deposits

Money can be invested in term deposits which yield an interest rate return. Generally there is minimum deposit of $1000 or $5000 and at least a 2 month investment period. Interest can be calculated annually, quarterly, monthly or even daily.

Calculating interest on money invested

To work out simple interest:

Principal amount × Interest rate/100 × Time in years
= Interest earned

For example: $5000 invested for 2 years has an interest rate of 3.0%. After 1 year there will be $150 in interest:

$5000   ×   3/100   = $150
principal amount   interest rate   interest earned

This simple interest can be taken, or can be added to the original amount (compound interest).

So after 2 years simple interest will result in $300 total interest.

$5000   ×   3/100   ×   2   = $300
principal amount   interest rate   time in years   interest earned

To work out compound interest:

Principal amount $(1 + \text{interest rate per time interval}/100)^{\text{number of time intervals}}$
= Total amount

Compound interest after two years will result in $304.50.

$5000   × $(1 + 3/100)^2$ = $5304.50
principal amount[1]   (1 + interest rate per time   total amount
                        interval/100)$^{\text{number of time intervals}}$

The longer money is left invested, the greater the return, although sometimes this money cannot be accessed earlier without paying a penalty.

Buying a car

As well as the purchase cost of the car there are extra items to take into consideration, such as:

- ◆ registration
- ◆ compulsory transport injury insurance
- ◆ comprehensive insurance
- ◆ government transfer fees and stamp duty
- ◆ dealer's delivery charge (for new car buyers only)
- ◆ number plate fee (new car buyers only)
- ◆ optional mechanical inspection (used car buyers)
- ◆ optional extras such as extended warranty

Note that these additional costs can vary considerably. For example, the cost of compulsory insurance will depend upon your driving history, the age of the youngest driver of the car and whether the car is to be used for business or private purposes.

Some indication of the range of costs is provided by the table below.

Item of expense	Applies to	Approximate cost range	Average cost
Registration	Car	$180–$220	$190
Compulsory insurance	Youngest driver aged 30 years, main driver has good driving history	$350–$380	$355
Comprehensive insurance	2003 sedan, agreed value $30,000. Youngest driver aged 30 years, main driver has good driving history	$650–$750	$700

Running costs

Information about the total running costs for a range of cars per week can be found on motoring websites such as NRMA (New South Wales) or the RACV (Victoria). The following table indicates the average costs for a typical Sports Utility Vehicle (SUV) model.

Standing costs – average cents/km	
Depreciation	35–45
Cost of funds	12–15
Registration, Comprehensive Insurance and Club Membership	8–9
Running costs – average cents/km	
Fuel	11–15
Tyres	1.2–1.5
Service and repairs	3.3–5.5
Total costs	
Average cents per kilometre	80–85
Average dollars per week	$230–$250

Fuel

The cost of fuel can vary from day to day and location to location.

Petrol prices can be observed on web sites for many Australian locations, for example www.aip.com.au.

Working out fuel costs

The amount of fuel required for a trip depends on many factors including engine size, travel distance, frequency of stops, load that is being carried and the quantity of fuel the particular vehicle can carry.

Engine size

Engine sizes vary in vehicles and this can determine the cost of your travel.

	Honda CRV	Toyota RAV4	Nissan X-Trail
Fuel Consumption			
Overall (Litres/100km)	10.1 L/100 km	10.6 L/100 km	10.4 L/100 km
Fuel Tank Capacity (litres)	58 litres	57 litres	60 litres

Source: *www.racv.com.au*

Let's look at some examples.

To estimate your total fuel cost:

Average cost of fuel in $ per km × Distance travelled = Total fuel cost

Example 1: A medium car, such as a Toyota Camry, has the approximate running fuel cost of 10.06¢ per km compared to a larger car, such as a V8 Ford Fairlane, which has the approximate fuel costs of 14.83¢ per km.

So for a trip covering 500km the approximate cost of fuel for the Fairlane would be:

0.1483	×	500	=	$74.15
average cost of fuel per km		distance travelled		total fuel cost

To estimate how often you will need to refuel:

Amount of fuel for trip ÷ Tank capacity
= Minimum number of times for refuelling

Because the tank of the CRV Honda only holds 58 litres it will be necessary to refuel at least twice.

121.32	÷	58	=	2.1
amount of fuel for trip		tank capacity		minimum number of times for refuelling

Travel time

Many factors affect how long a trip will take. In general, if you are travelling at 100km per hour and you are covering a distance of 100km, then the trip will take approximately 1 hour.

To estimate how long a trip will take:

Distance to travel/Speed × 60 = Approximate journey time in minutes

For example: If you have 25km to travel and you are travelling at 100km per hour, then it will take approximately 15 minutes.

25/100	×	60	=	15 minutes
distance to travel/speed		minutes (ie one hour)		approximate journey time

If you have 20 km to travel and your speed is 60km per hour, then it will take approximately 20 minutes.

20/60	×	60	=	20 minutes
distance to travel/speed		minutes (ie one hour)		approximate journey time

If you are travelling a longer distance, i.e. Melbourne to Mildura which is approximately 550km, you will need to allow more than the calculated time of approximately 5½ hours, due to the need to slow down through towns and for breaks. (It is recommended to break after every 90 minutes of driving.) There are web sites which enable you to calculate travel time, distances and the most efficient route to take, for example: *www.travelmate.com.au*

There are three basic ways to earn money – salary, wages or commission.

Salaries

Salaries are when a set amount per year is offered, i.e. $65 000. It can be paid monthly, fortnightly or weekly. Different organisations have different ways of calculating the rate. For example:

Calculating your salary

To calculate your salary:

Annual salary ÷ 313 × 12 = Fortnightly salary

Annual salary ÷ 313 × 12 ÷ 2 = Weekly Salary

Annual Salary ÷ 313 × 12 ÷ 70 (for 35-hour week staff)

or 76 (for 38-hour week staff) = Hourly rate

Note: This formula is devised on the basis that there are exactly 313 fortnights over a 12 year period.

For example: if a person is earning $65 000 per year, using the above formula, they would receive $2492.01 fortnightly before tax:

$65 000	÷	313 × 12	=	$2492.01
annual salary		fortnightly calculation		fortnightly salary

Wages

Wages are generally paid based on the number of hours worked and are paid to people whose hours vary from week to week, such as part-time or casual workers.

Calculating your weekly wage

To calculate your weekly wage:

Amount per hour × Number of hours worked = Weekly wage

For example: a worker earns $55.60 per hour and works 18.5 hours in a week, so the weekly wage would be $1028.60 before tax:

$55.60	×	18.5	=	$1028.60
amount per hour		hours worked		weekly wage

Wages are generally more per hour than a salary, because people earning wages may not be paid entitlements such as holiday pay or sick leave.

Commission

Commission is paid as a percentage of an item sold. Sometimes payment is purely 'on commission', other times it is linked to a wage/salary.

Working out commission

> To work out the commission:
> **$Amount of sales × Percentage of sales = Commission**

Example 1: a person selling kitchen items receives 20% of all sales, so if they sold $500 worth of product, they earn $100 commission.

$500	×	20/100	=	$100
$amount of sales		**percentage of sales**		**commission**

Example 2: there may be the opportunity of some passive advertising on a web site you own, and the commission rate is 4% on the total of products purchased. If $600 worth of product was sold, then you would receive $24.00 in total.

$600	×	4/100	=	$24
$amount of sales		**percentage of sales**		**commission**

Salary packaging

Salary packaging is an opportunity that some employers provide to help you reduce your income tax. Normally your employer would pay you in the form of a cash salary after tax deductions. You would then pay expenses such as motor vehicle lease repayments, lap top computer, mobile phone etc., from your after-tax salary. With salary packaging, you restructure your salary by choosing to take a percentage of your salary in cash and package-approved benefits on which you would pay fringe benefits tax. You should ensure that you have these arrangements in writing from your employer. (For more information on fringe benefits tax, see *Blake's Go Guide: Tax and You*.)

Calculating your taxable salary

> How to calculate your taxable salary:
> **Weekly pre-tax salary – Weekly cost of packaged item = Taxable salary**

For example: if your pre-tax salary was $1009.50 per week, and you salary packaged a car and its running costs at $350.00 per month (on average $80.77 per week).

$1009.50	–	$80.77	=	$928.73
weekly pre-tax salary		**weekly cost of packaged item**		**taxable salary**

Then you would pay income tax on $928.73 and fringe benefits tax on the balance (ie $80.77).

What items can be packaged

Items that may be included in a salary package are:

- Motor Vehicles & Running Costs
- Mortgage & Personal Loan Repayments
- Investment Loan Repayments
- Rental Payments Superannuation
- Child Minding Expenses
- School Fees
- Professional Development Expenses
- General Insurances
- Utility Expenses (e.g. gas, electricity, etc.).

Pay slip

A typical pay slip may include the following information:

Information		Example
Pay period	weekly/fortnightly/monthly	Fortnightly
Date of payment		27/11/03
Gross payment	Amount for that pay period. This may show the number of hours and amount paid per hour.	$750.26
YTD payment	Year to date total = previous YTD + base payment of this pay	$4501.56
Superannuation	This will be shown as an amount if paid by the employer and it will be deducted from the pre-tax total if an employee contribution.* Base payment × percentage super/100 = super contribution * Pre- or post-tax depends on whether salary sacrifice is used.	$67.52 (employer contribution (9%))
Tax	This is determined by the amount you earn** **See the information and table below	$88.32
YTD Tax	Year to date total = previous YTD + base payment of this pay	$529.88
Net pay	This is the actual amount you "take home".	$661.94

Note: other items such as reimbursements, annual leave accrual or HECS deductions may also be shown on the pay slip.

Tax rates
Individual

In Australia, a person's income is taxed progressively, which means the more you earn the more your average tax rate rises. This is achieved by taxing a range of income brackets as a set percentage or cents in the dollar (called tax brackets). The following table shows the tax brackets for the financial year ending 30 June 2004, as known at the time of publication.

The first bracket is known as the tax-free threshold and no tax is paid.

Tax rates 2003–04

Taxable income	Tax on this income
$0 – $6000	Nil
$6001 – $21 600	17c for each $1 over $6000
$21 601 – $52 000	$2652 plus 30c for each $1 over $21 600
$52 001 – $62 500	$11 772 plus 42c for each $1 over $52 000
Over $62 500	$16 182 plus 47c for each $1 over $62 500

Source: *www.ato.gov.au*

Note: The above rates do not include the Medicare levy of 1.5%.

Working out your total earnings

To calculate your total yearly earnings:
**Amount per pay period × Number of pay periods
= Total earnings**

A person earns $750.26 per fortnight and there are 26 fortnights in a year:

$750.26   ×   26   = $19 506.76
amount per pay period   number of pay periods   total earnings

Working out how much tax to pay

With a wage of $19 506.76, this person falls in the second tax bracket (see tax rates in the table above), and pays 17c for each dollar over $6000.

To work out your tax liability:
**Total annual earnings – Tax free threshold = Annual amount subject to tax
Annual amount subject to tax × Tax rate = Amount of tax
Annual amount of tax/Number of pay periods = Amount of tax
per pay period**

So they will pay tax on:

$19 506 .76	–	$6000	=	$13 506.76
total annual earnings		tax free threshold		annual amount subject to tax

Applying the rate (17¢/100):

$13 506.76	× 17¢/100	= $2296.15
annual amount subject to tax	tax rate	amount of tax

Now dividing this for a fortnight:

$2296.15	÷	26	=	$88.32
annual amount of tax		number of pay periods		amount of tax per pay period

Note: the Medicare levy and other tax liabilities (such as HECS repayments) will also need to be calculated to work out the total tax payable. See *Blake's Go Guide: Tax and You*.

Company income tax

A company is a distinct legal entity with its own income tax liability. A company must lodge a company tax return which shows the income and deductions of the company. This information is used to calculate the income tax that the company should pay. Deductions may be claimed for such things as salaries and wages, the cost of stock, rent, bad debts and previous year losses.

Calculating how much tax to pay

A company's income tax is calculated as a percentage of the taxable income earned by the company during the financial year. The company tax rate, as of the 2003–04 income year is 30%.

To calculate the amount of company tax to pay:

Total earnings – Total deductions = Income

Income × Applicable tax rate = Amount of tax to pay

For example: a small company has total earnings of $75 000 and deductions of $57 600. This leaves an income for the company of $17 400, and the amount of tax to be paid would be calculated as follows:

$17 400 ×	30/100	=	$5220
income	applicable tax rate		amount of tax to pay

Note: the final amount of tax to be paid can be reduced by any PAYG (Pay As You Go) instalments which are paid quarterly during the year based on the company's previous year's earnings.

SUPERANNUATION

Nearly every employed person must join a superannuation fund. Under the Superannuation Guarantee Charge your employer must contribute at least 9% of your earnings to the fund. The contribution is based on the ordinary hours of work and may include overtime. Superannuation can only be accessed when you permanently retire from the workforce and reach the minimum age set by law of 60 (although there are exceptions, for example ill health, death).

Working out your employer's contribution

To work out how much your employer is contributing:

Gross earnings × 9/100 = Employer super contribution

If you are earning $750.26 per week before tax, your employer would contribute $67.52 per week

$750.26 × 9/100 = $67.52
earnings   **the percentage**   **employer super contribution**

You may also contribute to superannuation, and you can vary this percentage.

Working out superannuation management fees

Each year, or more frequently, you will receive a statement from your superannuation company. There will be fees deducted from your superannuation, and these can be either a percentage of the money in the account or of the amount contributed. There will also be an ongoing management fee, charged as a percentage on the amount in the account.

To work out what the fund will charge to manage your super:

Amount in account × Management percentage/100 = Fee cost

Therefore if you have $10 000 in the account and the fees are 1%, this will cost you $100 per year,

$10 000 × 1/100 = $100
amount in account   **management percentage**   **fee cost**

The superannuation will be invested in one of the following types of funds – growth, balanced, capital stable or capital guaranteed, and these products will be offered by the company. Some investment choices are more unstable than others. Although a small investment can grow significantly over a period of time.

Working out how much a super fund will grow

How to work out how much your fund will grow:

Total amount = Starting amount

× (1 + rate per year/100) number of years

For example:
$10 000 invested at 4% per year for 20 years will result in approximately a total sum of $22 000.

$A = P(1 + r/100)^n$
$A = \$10\ 000\ (1 + 4/100)^{20}$
$A = \$21\ 911.23$

$A =$ Amount in total
$P =$ Principal (starting amount)
$r =$ Rate per year
$n =$ Number of years

Note: For most superannuation funds the rate of return will vary from year to year.

Working out the tax on your super

All employer contributions paid to superannuation funds are currently taxed at a maximum of 15%.

How to work out the tax component of your super contribution:

Total employer contributions × 15/100 = Tax paid

For example: if an employer contributed $810.24 per year, then the tax paid would be:

$810.24 × 15/100 = $121.54
total employer contributions **applicable tax rate** **tax paid**

If you take your superannuation as a <u>lump sum payment</u> when you retire, then you will pay a different rate of tax. This varies according to the different components that make up your ETP (Eligible Termination Payments). Some components may attract no tax, others may attract a marginal rate and some components may attract the highest marginal rate. The Medicare levy will be paid on any component that attracts tax.

GOODS AND SERVICES TAX (GST)

Introduced in Australia in 2000, the GST is a consumption tax. It requires businesses to charge GST at the rate of 10% on goods and services that they supply. Some items, such as exports, health, some food, education, international travel and certain charitable activities, are GST free.

A requirement in Australia is that GST be included in the final price and be clearly itemised on receipts. For example, a typical food shopping receipt may look like:

*Nappies	$12.95
Bread	$3.13
Lamb	$5.31
*Cola	$1.58
Onions	$1.89
Subtotal	$24.86
*Taxable items	
GST included in total	$1.32

Taxable items are denoted in some form, in this case by an asterix (*).

Calculating how much GST is included

The taxable items on the receipt above were the nappies and the cola, which total $14.53.

$12.95 + $1.58 = $14.53
nappies   cola   total price of purchases (including GST)

> To work out the original price before GST:
> **Current price × 10/11 = Original price before GST**

Hence the original price before the GST was added would be:
for the nappies

$12.95 × 10/11 = $11.77
current price   fraction   original price before GST

and for the cola

$1.58 × 10/11 = $1.44
current price   fraction   original price before GST

making a total of $13.21 before GST.

To work out the GST component:

Current price × 1/11 = GST component

And the GST component would be
for the nappies

$12.95 × 1/11 = $1.18
current price   fraction   GST component

for the cola

$1.58 × 1/11 = $0.14
current price   fraction   GST component

making a total of $1.32 GST for the two items and a total purchase price of $14.53.

Calculating GST in quotations

In some cases the price is quoted as not including GST.

To work out the GST inclusive price:

Original price + (Original price × 1/10) = Total price (including GST)

For example, a plumber is charging $500 plus GST to complete the repairs of a bathroom. The total price will be $550.

$500 + ($500 × 1/10) = $550
original price (original price × fraction) total price

Calculating the current price and the GST component

Sometimes it is necessary to quote both the original price and the GST.

To work out both the current price and the GST component

Price including GST × 1/11 = GST component

Price including GST × 10/11 = Original price

For example: an ink replacement cartridge is purchased for a printer at a cost of $44.50, and it is necessary for the original price and the GST to be stated separately for the purpose of tax. This could be calculated as follows:

$44.50 × 1/11 = $4.05
price including GST fraction GST component

$44.50 × 10/11 = $40.45
price including GST fraction original price

CURRENCY

The table below shows the value of one Australian dollar compared to the values of other currencies around the world. Current exchange rates can be found in major newspapers, on the Internet, and on the television news.

	Units of foreign currency per A$				
	13 May 2003	14 May 2003	15 May 2003	16 May 2003	19 May 2003
United States dollar	0.6487	0.6452	0.6438	0.6422	0.6564
Japanese yen	75.53	75.25	74.82	74.68	75.65
Euro	0.5619	0.5609	0.5629	0.5633	0.5616
New Zealand dollar	1.1233	1.1252	1.1245	1.1202	1.1224
UK pound sterling	0.4027	0.4011	0.3988	0.3963	0.4025

Source: Reserve Bank of Australia web site: *www.rba.gov.au*

Changing Australian dollars to another currency

To change Australian dollars to another currency:
The currency amount × The rate

For example:
For the United States on the 13 May 2003, the value is 0.6487. This means that one Australian dollar is equal to 0.6487 of the American dollar, so if you were to exchange one Australian dollar you would have approximately 65 cents of American currency. Therefore to exchange $300 Australian dollars to American dollars (excluding commissions and fees):

$300   ×   0.6487 = US$194.61
the currency amount   **the rate**

Changing another currency back to Australian dollars

To change another currency back to Australian dollars:

The currency amount ÷ The rate

For example:

If you were in Europe and wished to exchange your 500 Euro for Australian currency, on the 19 May 2003, the exchange rate was 0.5616.

500 Euro   ÷   0.5616 = A$890.31
the currency amount   the rate

Note: It is common for Exchange providers to charge a fee for these services.

UNDERSTANDING PERCENTAGES

Percentage means out of 100.

For example: 50/100 is 50 out of 100 or 0.5 or ½ or 50%.

For example: I have 90% of the biscuits left. 90% means that you have 90 biscuits out of 100 or 90/100 or 9/10.

Calculating the amount left to pay on a discount

To work out the amount to pay:

Total amount × Percentage discount = Amount of discount

Total amount − Amount of discount = Amount to pay

Example 1: At a sale there is 15% off all clothes. If I bought a top for $29.95, I would get a $4.49 discount.

$29.95   ×   15/100   = $4.49
total amount   percentage discount   amount of discount

I would pay $25.46 after the discount.

$29.95   − $4.49   = $25.46
total amount   amount of discount   amount to pay

Let's look at a second example.

Calculating a percentage decrease

To work out a percentage decrease:

Final amount/original amount × 100 = Percentage of original value

100 − Percentage of original value = Percentage decrease

Example 2: if I bought a new car for $24 000 and 4 years later it is worth only $15 000:

$15 000   / $24 000   × 100 =   62.5%
final amount original amount   percentage of original value

So the the car has decreased in value by 37.5%:

100%   −   62.5%   =   37.5%
percentage of original value   percentage decrease

Calculating the amount to pay when the price increases

To work out the amount to pay:

Total amount × Percentage increase = Amount of increase

Total amount + Amount of increase = Amount to pay

Example 1: For the top worth $29.95, if after the weekend its price increased by 5%, then:

$29.95   ×   5/100   = $1.50
total amount   **percentage increase**   **amount of increase**

I would then pay $31.45 after the increase.

$29.95   + $1.50   = $31.45
total amount   **amount of increase**   **amount to pay**

Let's look at another example:

To work out a percentage increase:

Final amount/Original amount × 100%

= Percentage of original value

Percentage of original value – 100% = Percentage increase

Example 2: If I bought a house in 1998 for $350 000 and sold it 5 years later for $560 000, then the percentage increase is:

$560 000   / $350 000   × 100 =   160%
final amount   **original amount**   **percentage of original value**

So the value of the house has increased by 60%.

160%   –   100%   =   60%
percentage of original value   **percentage increase**

Working out the discount

You may want to check a price, to ensure that you receive the correct discount.

To check or estimate the price:

25% is one-quarter

30% is approximately one-third

50% is half

65% is approximately two-thirds

75% is three-quarters

Total amount × Percentage discount = Amount of discount

Here are two examples:

Example 1: A shop has 40% off all Manchester. If the original cost of the item was $69.95, and you were charged $65.00 after the discount, it is obviously wrong – 40% is almost 50% or half, so the item should have been about $40. In fact:

$69.95   ×   40/100   = $27.98
total amount   **percentage discount**   **amount of discount**

$69.95   – $27.98   = $41.97
total amount   **amount of discount**   **amount to pay**

The price you should have paid was $41.97, so the estimate of $40 was very close.

Example 2: A toy costing $89.95 has 25% off, which is one-quarter. So approximating:

¼ of $90.00 is $22.50
Therefore the price is approximately:
$90.00   – $22.50   = $67.50
total amount   **approx discount**   **amount to pay**

The actual discount estimate was $67.50 compared to the real price of $67.46:

$89.95   ×   25/100   = $22.4875
total amount   **percentage discount**   **amount of discount**

$89.95   – $22.4875   = $67.46
total amount   **amount of discount**   **amount to pay**

Statistics

Statistics is the collection, organisation, presentation, interpretation and analysis of data. Statistics are used in many areas of everyday life including election results, polls, nutritional facts and sports information.

Understanding election results

The table below shows election results for the Canberra area, for all the represented parties/groups.

The first column is the different party/group. The column under the 'votes' heading is the number of votes received for that party. The percentage column is the percentage of the total number of votes received.

Generally, the total percentage should add up to 100%, but in the case of elections, some people vote incorrectly (informal vote) and some do not vote at all which leaves a shortfall in the total.

To work out voting shortfall:

Percentage of Formal votes + Percentage of Informal votes = 100%

For example: In the Brindabella area, with 64 020 people enrolled, the formal and informal percentages add to 100%,

$$\underset{\text{percentage of formal votes}}{95.52\%} + \underset{\text{percentage of informal votes}}{4.48\%} = 100\%$$

But, in fact, the total was only 92.56%, as it is the total number of votes out of the enrolment.

Working out percentage of votes

To work out the percentage of votes cast:

Total votes cast (Formal votes + Informal votes)/Total enrolment × 100 = Percentage of votes cast

$$\underset{\text{total of formal plus informal votes}}{\text{i.e. } 59\ 257} \Big/ \underset{\text{total enrolment}}{64\ 020} \times 100 = \underset{\text{percentage of votes cast}}{92.56\%}$$

Party/group	Brindabella Votes	%	Ginninderra Votes	%	Molonglo Votes	%	ACT Total Votes	%
AD	3938	6.96%	5408	9.71%	5992	7.63%	15338	8.04%
ALP	24891	43.97%	23852	42.82%	30873	39.31%	79616	41.72%
CFP	0	0.00%	0	0.00%	669	0.85%	669	0.35%
DR	0	0.00%	3126	5.61%	0	0.00%	3126	1.64%
GEP	0	0.00%	346	0.62%	744	0.95%	1090	0.57%
KIG	636	1.12%	0	0.00%	244	0.31%	880	0.46%
LDP	297	0.52%	1045	1.88%	531	0.68%	1873	0.98%
LP	18035	31.86%	15552	27.92%	26803	34.13%	60390	31.64%
NGGP	950	1.68%	704	1.26%	1109	1.41%	2763	1.45%
NPG1	128	0.23%	0	0.00%	0	0.00%	128	0.07%
NPG2	0	0.00%	469	0.84%	0	0.00%	469	0.25%
NPG3	0	0.00%	0	0.00%	284	0.36%	284	0.15%
NPG4	0	0.00%	0	0.00%	932	1.19%	932	0.49%
NPG5	0	0.00%	0	0.00%	478	0.61%	478	0.25%
PO	3888	6.87%	0	0.00%	0	0.00%	3888	2.04%
TAG	3074	5.43%	4426	7.94%	9869	12.57%	17369	9.10%

Party/group	Brindabella Votes	Brindabella %	Ginninderra Votes	Ginninderra %	Molonglo Votes	Molonglo %	ACT Total Votes	ACT Total %
UNG	767	1.36%	780	1.40%	0	0.00%	1547	0.81%
Formal	56604	95.52%	55708	95.98%	78528	96.33%	190840	95.99%
Informal	2653	4.48%	2336	4.02%	2985	3.66%	7974	4.01%
Total votes	59257	92.56%	58044	91.74%	81513	89.25%	198814	90.94%
Enrolment	64020		63267		91328		218615	

Source: *www.elections.act.gov.au*

Polls

Polls are another area of statistics related to politics. They provide a comparison between the major parties, and if an election was to be held, who would be likely win.

The table below, allows us to make a numerical comparison, and in this case the two figures always add up to 100%.

For example: For the 10 November 2001 election, the Liberal – National Party had 51% and the Australian Labor Party had 49% of the vote, i.e. 51% + 49% = 100%

TWO-PARTY PREFERRED VOTE	L-NP	ALP
Election March 2, 1996	53.6	46.4
Election October 3, 1998	49	51
Election November 10, 2001	51	49
MORGAN POLL 2003		
May 10/11 & May 17/18	50	50
May 24/25 & May 31/ June 1	47	53
June 7/8 & June 14/15	51	49
June 21/22 & June 28/29	51	49
July 5/6 & July 12/13	50.5	49.5

Source: *www.roymorgan.com*. Data used with permission of Roy Morgan Research

Consumer information

Statistics are also used to examine information, other than politics. The graph on the next page shows the percentage of households in Australia that have computers (green), as well as the percentage of households that have Internet access (orange) during the period February 1998 to November 2000. Therefore in February 2000, more than 40% of households had computers, and more than 20% had the Internet.

Household computer and Internet access

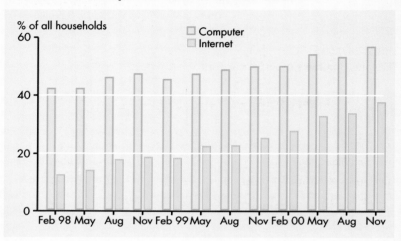

Source: *www.abs.gov.au* Data used with permission from the Australian Bureau of Statistics.

Nutritional facts

Nutritional facts are statistics and information that appear on the labels of all of our food. They provide us with information about the components which make up the food (both good and not so good).

For example: below is a table of nutritional facts for a popular spread.

Nutrients	Based on 100 grams of Peanut Butter
Fat	52.1 g
Protein	26.9 g
Carbohydrates	—Total 13.4 g —Sugars 9.6 g
Calcium	34 mg
Phosphorous	320 mg
Potassium	497 mg
Sodium	500 mg

To make comparisons it is important to have all the
quantities in the same units.

The table on the previous page shows that for every 100g serving there is
52.1g of fat (good and not so good) – this is more than half.
It also shows that there is 34mg of calcium.
This is 34/1000 = 0.034g of calcium in 100g.
The following table provides nutritional facts for a spread (5g).

% Proportion of Recommended Daily Intake (RDI)		
	Per 5g	**Per 100g**
Thiamine (Vitamin B1)	50%	13mg
Niacin (Vitamin B3)	25%	10.3mg
Riboflavin (Vitamin B2)	25%	9.2mg
Folate (C, E)	50%	2000µg
Iron	25%	10mg

This table shows percentages and per 100g values.
    The spread has 13.0mg Thiamine per 100g of product, which is
    13/1000 = 0.013g in 100g. And there is 2000µg of Folate, which is
    2000/1 000 000 = 0.002g in 100g.

SHOPPING

Working out the amount to be paid when an item is weighed

When shopping in a supermarket, items such as fruit, vegetables and deli items can be purchased in set packaging as per the rest of the supermarket or can be purchased by weight.

For example oranges could be purchased:

◆ in a 3kg bag for $4.98
◆ individually, say for 69¢ each
◆ by weight i.e. $1.66 per kilogram (kg). Hence 5kg would be 5 × $1.66 = $8.30.

Often it is cheaper to buy items pre-packaged or by the bag, however there is more choice for quality if each item is selected individually. Fruit and vegetables are normally weighed and the price calculated at the cash register. This price includes the weight of the packaging (which is generally negligible).

Deli items such as meats, cheeses and seafoods are selected by staff and most items are calculated either by weight or individually. The price is allocated in the section and attached to the package.

To work out the amount to be paid when an item is weighed:

Weight (in grams)/1000 × Cost per kg = Amount to be paid

For example: The cost of 250g of shaved ham at $9.95 per kg would be:

250g/1000 × $9.95   = $2.49
weight/1000   cost per kg   amount to be paid

Working out rounding

If payment is made by credit card, cheque or EFTPOS, then rounding doesn't apply and the exact totalled amount is charged. For cash payments, rounding is basically at the store's discretion, and they will round up or down to the nearest 5¢ or 10¢, based on the total price.

To round cents to the nearest amount:

Items that end in 1 or 2 will be rounded down to the nearest 10¢
Items that end in 6 or 7 will be rounded down to the nearest 5¢
Items that end in 3 or 4 will be rounded up to the nearest 5¢
Items that end in 8 or 9 will be rounded up to the nearest 10¢

For example:

- **$27.51 or $27.52** will be **rounded down** to $27.50
  end in 1   end in 2   nearest 10c
- **$27.53 or $27.54** will be **rounded up** to $27.55
  end in 3   end in 4   nearest 5c
- **$27.56 or $27.57** will be **rounded down** to $27.55
  end in 6   end in 7   nearest 5c
- **$27.58 or $27.59** will be **rounded up** to $27.60
  end in 8   end in 9   nearest 10c

Discount and reward programs

There is a wealth of discount programs entering the market regarding general shopping. Some of the more common ones include shareholder discounts, Fly Buys and Community cards.

Working out shareholder discounts

This card allows shareholders owning a certain number of shares to receive discounts within the stores or on certain items.

To work out the price after discount:

Full price × Percentage discount /100 = Amount of discount

Full price − Amount of discount = New price to be paid

For example: A Sports Store offers shareholders with 2000 shares a 7.5% discount on all non-sale merchandise.

A shareholder wishes to purchase a pair of shoes valued at $250.

$250   ×   7.5/100   = $18.75
full price   percentage discount/100   amount of discount

The cost of the shoes after the discount is $231.25

$250   − $18.75   = $231.25
full price   amount of discount   new price to be paid

Working out the number of points for Fly Buys

Programs such as Fly Buys allow card holders to receive 1 point for every $5 spent at certain shops, on showing the card. Points can be redeemed for a range of items including electrical items, toys, wine, vouchers etc. There are also bonus offers made from time to time.

To work out the number of points:

Total spent/Amount per point = Number of points

For example: If $132.95 has been spent at the sports store, and the card holder receives 1 point for every $5 spent, then the cardholder would receive 26.59 points:

$$132.95 \quad / \quad 5 \quad = \quad 26.59$$

total spent   **amount per point**   **number of points**

Note: Part points are not awarded, so the total number of point received would be 26.

Working out amount for donations on Community cards

If you shop at a certain store and buy certain products, the store puts aside a set amount from each of these products sold. At the end of each year, local groups or charities receive this money as a donation.

How to work out the amount for donation:

Number of items × Amount = Amount for donation

For example: If 54 products had been purchased and 1¢ was donated from each product, then 54¢ would be donated to charity.

Working out the amount left on Lay-by

Lay-by is often offered in stores on total purchases over a certain price. A deposit is normally required and sometimes there is a service fee. Items are held for a certain period of time, with regular payments required.

Total cost × Percentage of deposit/100 = Deposit

Deposit + Service fee = First payment

Remaining total/Number of payments = Amount to paid each time

For example: Lay-by could be offered under the following conditions. It is available on any purchases of $20 or more with a 10% deposit and a $1.50 service fee. Goods will be held for eight weeks, with fortnightly payments. Purchases will be forwarded or available for collection on receipt of final payment.

For a bike, valued at $329.50 and placed on lay-by under the above conditions, the deposit would be $32.95.

$$329.50 \times \quad 10/100 \quad = 32.95$$

total cost   **percentage of deposit**   **deposit**

Then the service fee would need to be added.

$$32.95 + 1.50 \quad = \quad 34.45$$

deposit   **service fee**   **first payment**

The remaining total of $295.05

$329.50 – $32.95 = $296.55
total cost   first payment   remaining total

is then divided into the fortnightly payments over 8 weeks,

$296.55 / 4 = $74.14
remaining total no of payments   amount to be paid each time

Working out discounts

Often stores offer discounts, which are presented in a variety of ways. These include: 15% off store wide, 25% off a particular item, a dollar reduction amount, and buy 2 items and get one free.

If a store offers an amount off store-wide, it will be calculated on your total purchase.

> How to calculate discount amount:
>
> **Total cost × Percentage discount/100 = Discount amount**
>
> **Total cost – Discount amount = Amount to be paid**

For example: If the total cost of buying 3 DVDs is $91.85, and the discount is 15% off store-wide, the total cost is:

$91.85 × 15/100 = $13.78
total cost percentage discount   discount amount

$91.85 – $13.78 = $78.07
total cost   discount amount   amount to be paid

If the discount is on a certain item, either as a percentage or as a dollar reduction amount, this will only be calculated on the item itself. Most major stores can now complete this mid-transaction, so this amount will be itemised on a receipt. At other stores, discount items may be calculated at the start or at the end of the purchase. For an example the receipt may look like:

* Toy	12.95
* Book	5.15
* Manchester	5.31
DISC 20.0%	1.06 –
* Ink Cartridge	29.95
Total	52.30
* Taxable items	
GST included in total	4.75

The discount on the Manchester item is calculated by:

$5.31 × 20/100 = $1.06
total cost **percentage discount** **discount amount**

So the item would now cost $4.25:

$5.31 − $1.06 = $4.25
total cost **discount amount** **amount to be paid**

Working out the real cost of hire purchase

Hire purchase is an agreement between a company and the 'hirer', which allows the hirer to possess and use an item of equipment in return for regular payments. When the final payment is made the ownership of the goods is transferred to the hirer.

There are many advantages and disadvantages to this system. The advantages include: repayment schedules are flexible, the use of the goods is immediate with minimal amount of cash outlay, interest rates are fixed on the amount being financed and there may be a tax benefit. The hirer needs to be aware that an establishment fee applies, costs may apply if the contract is broken and hire purchase agreements are subject to GST.

How to work out the real cost of hire purchase:

Payment per month × 12 = Total payment per year

Payment per year × Number of years = Total amount paid

Total amount paid + Deposit = Full cost of item

An example may be the hire purchase of a computer, scanner and printer, which would cost $3496 normally. A deposit of $500 is paid, and $121.95 is paid per month. At the end of the three-year period, the computer is owned by the hirer at a cost of:

$121.95 × 12 = $1463.40
payment per month **no of months** **total payment per year**

$1463.40 × 3 = $4390.20
payment per year **no of years** **total amount paid**

$4390.20 + $500 = $4890.20
total amount paid **deposit** **full cost of item**

So the equipment costs a total of $4890.20 over the three years.

Buy now – pay later!

Sometimes outlets offer the promotion of 'Buy now – pay later!' where it is possible to sign a contract to enable the goods to be taken immediately and the amount paid later, i.e. 6 months, 12 months or even 2 years. If the amount is not paid by that time, large interest rates are imposed while the loan is paid off. Failure to do so may result in repossession of the goods and a resulting poor credit record.

Credit cards
Working out how much interest you owe

Credit cards are provided by banks and money lenders, and the majority are aligned with VISA, Bankcard or Mastercard.

Most credit cards have an annual fee, ranging from $0 to $150 and an interest-free period of between 44 and 55 days. Some credit cards have a credit limit, for example $300 or $8000, and if the credit card is not paid off in the interest-free period, then interest of between 14.50% to 18% per annum is charged. To encourage you to get a credit card some institutions use incentives, such as waiving the annual fee or giving you lower interest rates for the first 6 months. Many cards have reward programs linked to them.

Let's look at some examples:

To work out how much interest you owe:

Amount owed × Interest rate per month/100 = Interest charged

Example 1: Your VISA card has annual fee of $59.00 and a limit of $2000, with an interest rate of 16.15% per annum and up to 55 days interest free. You have purchased $1526.35 worth of items using your card and are due to pay off the card by 30 May. If you place $1527.00 on the card on the 30 May, then no interest will be charged because all the debt is paid off; in fact you would have 65¢ credit.

Example 2: If you still had $101.25 owing on the card on 30 May, you will be charged interest of $1.35,

$101.25   ×   16.15/12/100   = $1.35
amount owed   **interest rate per month/100**   **interest charged**

Working out how much money you owe

To work out the new total owed:
Amount owed + Interest charged = New total owed

For the example above:

$101.25   + $1.35   = $102.60 on the card
amount owed   **interest charged**   **new total owed**

Example 3: If you owe $1265.35 on the card and only pay off $600.00 in May, instead of the full amount, then you will owe the balance plus $8.75 in interest:

$1256.35   – $600.00   = $656.35
$656.35   ×   16.15/12/100   = $8.83
$656.35   + $8.83   = $665.18
amount owed   **interest charged**   **new total owed**

So at the start of June you would owe $665.18 on the card.

Working out the minimum amount

Most credit card statements have a minimum amount to be paid by the due date. The minimum amount is usually the interest owed for one month.

To work out the minimum amount:
Total owing × Interest rate per month/100 = Minimum amount

For example: If you owe $1526.35 on your card on 25 May,

$1526.35   ×   16.15/12/100   = $20.54
total owing   **interest rate per month**   **minimum amount**

If you still owed $20.40 from April then your minimum payment would be: $20.54 + $20.40 = $40.94

Note: the credit component and the cash component (cash advances) are charged at different interest rates.

Working out the penalty for late payment

If you do not pay the minimum amount you will possibly be charged a missed payment charge (usually about $25.00) and may receive a phone call from the bank.

Therefore a credit card could cost you as little as an annual fee or it can add up quickly if you do not pay the amount owing in time.

PHONE CALLS AND THE INTERNET

There are many options – local, STD, overseas, not to mention the wide variety of mobile plans. There are also many options for the Internet and e-mail including phone lines, ADSL, satellite and cable. When establishing what company or plan is the best value, it is worth spending time making note of your main uses and needs and shopping around. Many companies now offer complete packages, which include phone, mobile, fax and Internet access, as well as separate bills, or all the information and costs on the same bill.

Local and STD calls

There are two main national carriers for telephone calls, Telstra and Optus. Both offer a wide range of plans and special deals that are constantly being updated or changed. There are also smaller carriers, which are generally located in smaller regions.

Local calls vary from 17.5¢ to 22¢ per call, depending on the plan. There are also monthly access fees costing between $20.00 and $29.90 or line rental costs, of approximately $27.00. Call costs will probably vary if calling mobile phones or 1300 numbers; for example charges to mobile phones may be between $1.50 and $3.00 per minute.

STD calls within Australia, generally attract a per minute cost, ranging from 11¢ to 25¢ per minute. The time of the day affects the costs, so calls made after a certain time will be at the 11¢ end, while the more expensive costs will be during the day at peak rate. Some plans offer a capping system.

A typical phone bill summary may look like this:

Call Charges	Number of calls	Cost of calls	Cost + GST
Local calls	43 calls	7.74	8.51
Calls to 13 numbers	8 calls	1.82	2.00
STD calls	54 calls	68.28	75.11
Information calls	5 calls	1.33	1.46
Calls direct to mobiles	15 calls	9.50	10.45
Line rental plan		67.89	74.68
Total		**$156.56**	**$172.21**

Note: STD, calls to 13 numbers, information calls and calls to mobiles are itemised as part of the bill, so the amount per call can be noted.

Working out the total call cost

How to work out the total call cost:

Number of minutes × Cost per minute = Total call cost

For example: A call from Mildura to Melbourne lasting 27 minutes 40 seconds cost $15.32,

27.6 × 0.67¢ = $15.32
number of minutes   cost per minute   total call cost

International calls

International calls attract a connection fee of approximately 33¢. Calls are then charged at a rate per minute, although this depends on any plan or special offers. Often international calls are capped at a certain cost per period of time, so instead of paying 67¢ per minute, it is possible to pay $16.50 per half an hour.

For example:

½ hour at 67¢ per minute costs $20.10

30 × 0.67¢ = $20.10
number of minutes   cost per minute   total call cost

1/2 hour at $16.50 flat fee costs $16.50. This is a saving of $3.60.

Note: the same charge exists for each 1/2 hour block or part thereof and will exclude calls to some services such as international mobile numbers, pagers, and voicemail in some destinations.

Some examples of call costs are:

- 33¢ per minute to Italy
- 34¢ per minute to Hong Kong
- 75¢ per minute to China
- 21¢ per minute to the UK
- 21¢ per minute to the US
- 75¢ per minute to Turkey

Note: these costs depend on the carrier and the plan

Hence a 55 minute call to Turkey would cost $41.25,

55 × 0.75¢ = $41.25
number of minutes   cost per minute   total call cost

At the flat rate of $18.75 per half hour, the call cost would be $37.50, a saving of $3.75.

The Internet

There are four main ways to access the Internet – the phone line, cable, ADSL and satellite.

Phoneline packages

These packages offer users a pay per month system, based on the number of hours the Internet is used or the quantity of download materials. Often bonuses are included, such as free hours, technician support or free web space.

Working out annual cost

To work out the annual cost:

Cost per month × Number of months = Total cost

For example:

A low frequency user could pay $5.95 per month, as they use the Internet for less than 2 hours per month.

A high frequency user could pay $34.95 per month, and that would allow them to download a maximum of 700MB.

There is also the option of pre-paid, which may enable a user to use the Internet for 6 hours over 30 days or enable a user to use the Internet for 60 hours over 90 days for the cost of $54.95.

Working out total cost including extra hours

To work out the total cost including extra hours:

Cost per month × Number of months + (Cost per hour × Number of extra hours) = Total cost

If the use exceeds the plan by, say, 10 hours, charges are normally quite high. For example, the hourly rate may be $3.95 per hour (or 20¢ per MB).

$34.95 $\quad$ × $\quad$ 12 $\quad$ + $\qquad$ ($3.95 $\quad$ × $\quad$ 10) $\quad$ = $458.90
cost per month $\quad$ number of months $\quad$ cost per hour $\quad$ number of hours $\quad$ total annual cost

Cable packages

Cable packages have an installation fee based on use over a number of months. For example, the user could pay $189.00 for 18 months or $399.00 for 3 months. Then an additional amount per month is paid dependent on usage. For example, a user could pay $54.95 per month and be able to download up to 500MB or they could pay up to $305.95 per month and be able to download up to 10GB.

Working out the total cost

To work out the total cost:

Installation fee + (Cost per month × Number of months) = Total cost

This system of paying for installation and then paying a set amount per month also applies to <u>ADSL</u>. (ADSL is the system that allows the access of Broadband Internet without tying up the phone lines.) Installation fees range from $129.00 for 18 months up to $519.00 for 3 months for a 4 port modem. The payments per month range from $59.95 per month allowing the user to download up to 500MB, through to $329.95 per month allowing the user to download 10GB.

Satellite Internet

Satellite Internet has two options, one way which allows high-speed downloads and dial-up for uploads or two way. Both options attract equipment and installation fees, as well as a monthly charge. These costs are dependent on equipment, location, usage and other packages.

All the above costings and information can vary, due to special offers, plans and packages. These are examples only and up-to-date information should be accessed.

Telstra's website: *www.telstra.com*

Optus' website: *www.optus.com.au*

MOBILE CALLING

There are many options with mobile phones, with three main types of mobile phone plans and access:

1 pre-paid (no plan)
2 pay-as-you-go (variety of plans)
3 based on the amount of calls made.

The <u>pre-paid option</u> enables the user to have a mobile phone and pre-pay a set amount. This amount can range from $20.00 upwards and is topped up when the amount starts to become low. The user must purchase a phone, and the recharge card has an expiry time, e.g. 3 months.

Working out the cost of a pre-paid plan

On the pre-paid plan:

◆ A mobile phone is purchased for $199.00. (More expensive phones may include the SIM card.)
◆ The recharge SIM card is purchased for $30.00
◆ Calls cost 28¢ per 30 seconds.
◆ Text messages cost 20¢ per message.

To work out the total cost of a pre-paid phone plan:

Cost of phone + Cost of pre-paid card = Total cost

So the total cost to set up and start using the phone would be $229.00:

$199.00   + $30.00   = $229.00
cost of phone   cost of pre-paid card   **total cost**

Note: with all mobile phone calls there is a 'flagfall', which is a minimum amount to pay per call, and this is generally around the 20¢ mark.

Working out the cost of a pay-as-you-go plan

The pay-as-you-go options are countless. This type of plan generally includes a phone for free (or at very low cost). A set amount is paid per month and this is over a contract period of anything from 12–24 months, hence a minimum amount is paid. Cost penalties are applied for breaking the contract early. Call costs vary depending on the plan and the time of the day. Some of the special offers that may come with the plan include:

- call credit amounts
- cheaper SMS calls
- cheaper or even free calls to phones on the same plan after a certain time of the day or night
- cheaper overseas rates
- free hardware such as ear pieces, car chargers
- free delivery.

Some examples of costs from a range of companies are:

Per month	Flat rate (per 30 seconds)	Flagfall
$10.00	18¢	22¢
$10.00	50¢	20¢
$15.00	51.7¢	24.2¢
$18.00	28¢	22¢
$28.00	22¢	28¢
$33.00	44¢	24.2¢
$55.00	26.4¢	22¢
$77.00	23.1¢	22¢
$99.00	20.9¢	18.7¢
$150.00	18.7¢	18.7¢
$250.00	17.6¢	18.7¢
$350.00	18¢	20¢

Note: these costs will vary depending on the type of plan, when the calls are made and if they are affected by any special deals.

SMS messages vary in price and are approximately 25¢ per message.

To work out the total cost of a pay-as-you-go phone plan:

Cost per month + (Number of calls × Cost per call) + (Number of SMS × cost per SMS) = Total cost

For example: the access fee for the phone may be $10.00 per month, and you make 20 calls at a total cost of $18.60 and 10 SMS messages at $2.50, your total cost would be:

$10   + $18.60   + $2.50   = $31.10
cost per month   cost per 20 calls   cost of SMS   total cost

You can use a mobile phone when making international calls. Some examples of prices are:

$3.00 for 10 minutes to call London, Los Angeles, New York and New Zealand.
$4.00 for 10 minutes to call Hong Kong and Singapore.

When travelling overseas you can also use your mobile phone, although costs will vary greatly and sometimes it may be cheaper to purchase a pre-paid system in the country of travel.

   Some plans allow the user to pay the cost of the calls independent of the <u>number of calls made</u> in a particular month. This allows flexibility for the user, although a minimum amount must be spent. For example:

Your actual spend in a month	Your rate that month	Billed by the Second! Quoted per 30 secs	
		Off peak	Peak time
Over $50	Reduced rate	23c	35c
Up to $50	Talk up to $50	25c	45c
Over $100	Reduced rate	19c	22c
Up to $100	Talk up to $100	23c	35c
Over $200	Reduced rate	15c	20c
Up to $200	Talk up to $200	19c	22c

Source: *www.virginmobile.com.au*

A mobile phone account will look very similar to a normal phone account. For example:

Call Charges			
	Number of calls	**Cost of calls**	Cost + GST
Calls	29 calls	20.55	22.61
SMS	11 calls	2.50	2.75
Service calls	0 calls	0	0
	Total call charges	23.05	25.36
Access fee		10.00	11.00
Total		**$33.05**	**$36.36**

Again, individual calls and SMS would be itemised at the end of the bill. This information has been collected from the following sources:

Optus: *www.optus.com.au*
Orange: *www.orange.net.au*
Telstra: *www.telstra.com*
Virgin: *www.virginmobile.com.au*
Vodafone: *www.vodafone.com.au*

TIME

Clocks

There are two different types of time presentation used; 12 hour am and pm, and the 24-hour clock. Typically the 12 hour clock is used. For example:

◆ The TV program starts at 8:30pm.
◆ The train leaves at 7:58am.

Often a 24-hour clock is used, when the system is based on computers or the event runs 24 hours a day, like a fire station.

> To work out how the 24-hour clock is used:
>
> **Prior to 12pm: am time with a zero placed in front = 24-hour time**
> **After 12pm: pm time + 12 = 24-hour time**

To calculate the time in 24 hours, for example

◆ the train leaves at 07:58.
◆ the flight leaves at 8:40pm, which is:

8:40   + 12 =   20:40
pm time + 12 = 24 hour time

Here is a sample of some flight times:

| 02 Jul | Melbourne (MEL) | 19:10 | Mildura (MQL) | 20:30 |
| 03 Jul | Mildura (MQL) | 19:20 | Melbourne (MEL) | 20:40 |

How to go from 24 hour time to am/pm time

> To work out how to go from 24-hour time to am/pm time:
> **24 hour time (after 12:00) − 12 = pm time**

For example: The flight leaves Melbourne at 19:10, (which is 19:10 − 12:00 = 7:10pm) from Melbourne, and it arrives in Mildura at 20:30 which is:

20:30   − 12:00 = 8:30pm
24 hour time   (after 12:00) − 12.00 = pm time

Time differences

Given that the world is round, it follows that at any instant some people somewhere are sleeping while others elsewhere are eating lunch. In order to offer some consistency around the world, the world has been divided into 24 sections. Each section representing a time zone and adopting one of the day's 24 hours. Greenwich (in Great Britain) is taken as the reference time zone (also known as Greenwich Mean Time, GMT). In this way, the time zone directly east of Greenwich is 1 hour in advance while the time zone to the west of Greenwich is 1 hour later and so on for all the others.

Working out the time difference

The difference between the GMT variation of two locations
= Time difference

Let's look at two examples:

In the map of Australia below, it can be seen that for the East Coast of Australia, the time is GMT + 10 hours.

Example 1: To calculate the time in London (which is GMT +1, see the table on the following page) while in Sydney, it would be the time in Sydney minus 9 hours. So, if it was 11:00am in Sydney it would be 02:00am in London.

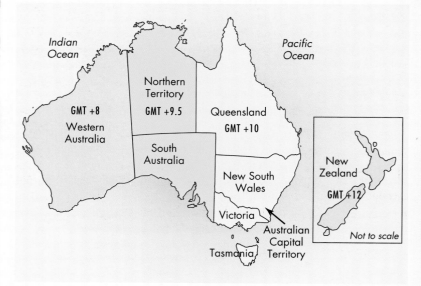

Example 2: Using the table on the following page, to calculate the time difference between two locations, for example: Sydney and Wellington, the difference is taken between the two variations from GMT. In this case 12 – 10 = 2 hours time difference.

Below is a list of time differences from GMT, and an example of the times in different locations:

GMT	Saturday	21 June, 2003	02:18 AM		
Athens	Saturday	21 June, 2003	05:18 AM	GMT + 0300	DST
Bangkok	Saturday	21 June, 2003	09:18 AM	GMT + 0700	
Berlin	Saturday	21 June, 2003	04:18 AM	GMT + 0200	DST
Cairo	Saturday	21 June, 2003	05:18 AM	GMT + 0300	
Dublin	Saturday	21 June, 2003	03:18 AM	GMT + 0100	DST
Hong Kong	Saturday	21 June, 2003	10:18 AM	GMT + 0800	
Jerusalem	Saturday	21 June, 2003	05:18 AM	GMT + 0300	DST
London	Saturday	21 June, 2003	03:18 AM	GMT + 0100	DST
Los Angeles	Friday	20 June, 2003	07:18 PM	GMT - 0700	DST
Melbourne	Saturday	21 June, 2003	12:18 PM	GMT + 1000	
Moscow	Saturday	21 June, 2003	06:18 AM	GMT + 0400	DST
New York	Friday	20 June, 2003	10:18 PM	GMT - 0400	DST
Paris	Saturday	21 June, 2003	04:18 AM	GMT + 0200	DST
Rome	Saturday	21 June, 2003	04:18 AM	GMT + 0200	DST
Seoul	Saturday	21 June, 2003	11:18 AM	GMT + 0900	
Sydney	Saturday	21 June, 2003	12:18 PM	GMT + 1000	
Tokyo	Saturday	21 June, 2003	11:18 AM	GMT + 0900	
Vancouver	Friday	20 June, 2003	07:18 PM	GMT - 0700	DST
Wellington	Saturday	21 June, 2003	02:18 PM	GMT + 1200	

Note: DST stands for Daylight Savings Time which needs to be taken into account with the time differences.

There are many web sites which calculate the time differences including:
www.whitepages.com.au
www.aol.com.au/html/timezones

CALCULATOR TIPS

A standard calculator generally looks similar to the following:

Some useful information for the use of the calculator:

◆ The number keys and addition, subtraction, multiplication and division symbols work as per normal maths equations.
◆ The (C) clears all information.
◆ The (CE) clears the last entered information.
◆ The (M+) means that you are adding the information on the screen to the memory.

For example:

If you completed the equation: 2 × 15 = 30 and pressed (M+) the 30 would be stored in the memory. It would be indicated on the screen, with an indicative symbol, i.e. a M in the top right corner.

If you then completed the equation: 3 × 25 = 75 and again pressed (M+), this information would be added to the memory.

You could check the total, by pressing MR which will show you 105.

This information will be stored in the memory, until it is cleared.

◆ The (MR) means that you are recalling the information.
This shows you the total in the memory (105 in the above example).
◆ Once the information has been recalled to the screen it can be cleared with the (Min) or (MC) or (M–)

To clear the information from the memory, for the example above:

Press (MR) which means you will see 105.

Now press (Min) or (MC) or (M–) and this will clear the memory, and the indicative symbol will disappear.

You will then need to clear the screen as per normal.

◆ The (+/–) allows you to use negative numbers.

For example: if you were adding up a balance sheet, where the items in were positive and the items out were negative, then you could use this button.

i.e. 140 + 120 + (-150) + 121 = 231

◆ The (y^x) allows you to use numbers with powers. (It is not available on all calculators.)

For example: if you were calculating the area of a square floor, 5m x 5m, then you could use the calculator for $5^2 = 25$.

USEFUL INFORMATION

Table of prefixes

giga,	(G),	meaning 10^9	1000 000 000	e.g. 1 gigabyte of memory in the computer
mega,	(M),	meaning 10^6	1 000 000	e.g. 1 megatonne of explosives
kilo,	(k),	meaning 10^3	1 000	e.g. a kilogram of oranges
deci,	(d),	meaning 10^{-1}	1/10	e.g. a decilitre of medicine
centi,	(c),	meaning 10^{-2}	1/100	e.g. the tile is 20 square centimetres
milli,	(m),	meaning 10^{-3}	1/1000	e.g. the width of the window is 1200 millimetres

Units of length

10 millimetres (mm)	= 1 centimetre (cm)
10 centimetres	= 1 decimetre (dm) = 100 millimetres
100 centimetres	= 1 metre (m) = 1000 millimetres
10 metres	= 1 decametre (dam)
1000 metres	= 1 kilometre (km) = 1000 metres

Some common conversions

Begin with	Formula	To find
Inches	× 2.54	Centimetres
Feet	× 0.3048	Metres
Yard	× 0.9144	Metres
Miles	× 1.609	Kilometres
Pounds	× 0.4536	Kilograms
Degrees Fahrenheit (F)	(F – 32) × 5/9 = °C	Degrees Celsius (C)
Degrees Celsius (C)	(C × 1.8) + 32 = °F	Degrees Fahrenheit (F)
Gallon	× 3.785	Litres

There are a number of web sites where you can find easy conversion programs. One of these is *www.foxaustralia.com.au/conversion.shtml*.

INDEX